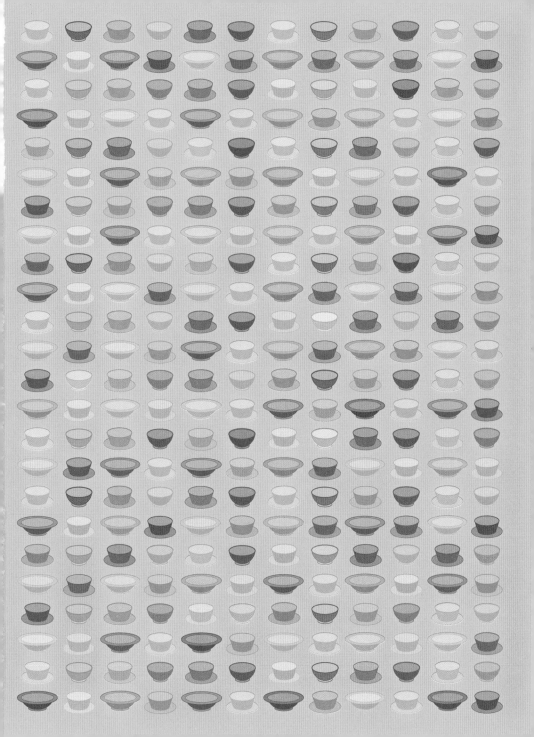

Penguin
Random
House

Writer Kate Turner

Senior Editor Ruth O'Rourke-Jones

Senior Art Editor Alison Gardner

Nutritionist Joy Skipper

Jacket Designer Harriet Yeomans

Jacket Editor Libby Brown

Pre-production Producer
Catherine Williams

Print Producer Stephanie McConnell

Creative Technical Support
Sonia Charbonnier

Photography Will Heap

Managing Editor Dawn Henderson

Managing Art Editor
Marianne Markham

Art Director Maxine Pedliham

Publishing Director Mary-Clare Jerram

First published in Great Britain in 2016

By Dorling Kindersley Limited,
80 Strand, London WC2R ORL

Copyright © 2016 Dorling Kindersley
A Penguin Random House Company

2 4 6 8 10 9 7 5 3 1
001 - 299214 - Oct/16

ISBN: 978-0-2412-8646-3

Printed and bound in China

**Discover more at
www.dk.com**

POWERbowls

ALL YOU NEED IN ONE HEALTHY BOWL

Contents

Breakfast
page 16

Quinoa & berry
porridge
page 18

Black rice
& tropical fruit bowl
page 20

Savoury oatmeal
power bowl
page 22

Ancient grains
porridge with pear
page 26

 Oatmeal bowls **page 24**

Acai berry & kale
smoothie bowl
page 28

Raw buckwheat &
blueberry bowl
page 30

Lunch on the go
page 32

Vegetarian sushi
bowl
page 34

Cauliflower rice
tabouli bowl
page 36

Ahi poke bowl
with seaweed salad
page 38
🥢 *Poke bowls* **page 40**

Tofu & kimchi
bowl
page 42

Buckwheat
& baba ganoush
page 44

Tex-Mex salad
& sweetcorn salsa
page 46

Millet Buddha bowl
with beetroot houmous
page 48

Dinner
page 50

Roasted roots
& pulses bowl
page 52

Steamed vegetables
& halloumi
page 54

Buckwheat pho
mushroom & mackerel
page 56
🥢 *Pho bowls* **page 58**

Spicy harissa chicken
& rice bowl
page 60

Courgetti
& roasted chickpeas
page 62

Spiced millet
& vegetable bowl
page 64

Grilled salmon teff
& vegetable ribbons
page 66

Spicy black bean
burrito bowl
page 68

What is a power bowl?

A power bowl is a nutritionally complete and totally balanced meal in one bowl. Whether it's a quick and easy breakfast for the family, a workday lunch for one, or a leisurely weekend dinner with friends, these bowls are full of flavour, bursting with colour, and brilliantly simple.

Here's how

Take one beautiful bowl, fill it with super-healthy ingredients, and make it look amazing. Then sit back and enjoy eating a meal that's packed with nutrient-dense foods and masses of natural energy to help power you through your day.

Superfood ingredients

All the recipes in this book focus on fresh fruits and vegetables, healthy whole grains, lean proteins, nuts, seeds, and nutri-boosting superfoods. They are naturally free of gluten and refined sugars with loads of variations to

Colour – pile on fruit
and veg for loads of
vitamins and minerals

Base – grains
and pulses to keep
you energized

Crunch – nuts and
seeds for extra
protein and texture

inspire you and help you make the
recipes your own. Eating in this way can
bring awesome health benefits, including
increased energy levels, improved moods,
greater ability to concentrate, and may
even help you to get a sounder night's
sleep to leave you feeling recharged. Every
delicious power bowl recipe is packed
full of superfood vitality to make you feel
fantastic and fill you with "get up and go"!

Protein – keeps you feeling full
and helps your body to repair

"...a nutritionally complete
& totally balanced meal in one bowl..."

Building a **power bowl**

There are so many ways to create the perfect power bowl. Layer up with
grains, veggies, nuts, seeds, tasty dressings, and a power-packed protein source
for a balanced and complete meal in one bowl. Choose the best quality
– preferably organic – ingredients for maximum health and vitality.

1. Base   2. Protein   3. Veggies or fruit

Start with a high-energy
base layer, such as
the lentils used here.
Whole grains, pulses,
and noodles
are awesome.

+

Add protein-rich
chickpeas (as above), fish,
eggs, or tofu. Mixing
grains and pulses provides
a complete plant-based
protein.

+

Pile on colourful raw or
cooked veggies, such as
carrots, kale, beetroot,
sweet potato, celeriac, and
rocket – all full of
vitamins.

Sunday prep
Read the recipes thoroughly and plan ahead. Make dressings, soak, chop, and marinate at the weekend to save time during a busy week.

"Pre-soak pulses, grains, nuts, and seeds to maximize their nutritional benefits."

4. Crunchy toppings

5. Dressing

+ Add extra crunch and texture with a sprinkling of nuts and seeds, such as walnuts and pumpkin seeds.

+ Finish off with a dressing. This one is made from honey, olive oil, and wholegrain mustard.

= **Tuck in and power up!**

Power ingredients

The best way to ensure a great-tasting power bowl is to use quality ingredients. Source fresh, seasonal, local, and organic produce for maximum benefits. These are some of our favourite nutrient-dense superfood ingredients.

Grains & pulses

Amaranth Rich in vitamins A and C, fibre, calcium, potassium, iron, and all nine essential amino acids, amaranth can protect against heart disease and lower blood pressure.

Beans and peas When combined with a grain, such as brown rice, beans and peas provide a complete plant-protein source that is on a par with meat.

Buckwheat Gluten-free buckwheat has high levels of vitamins, minerals, and fibre. It keeps the body fuelled with slow-release energy.

Lentils A great source of plant protein, lentils are also high in fibre, magnesium, potassium, and folate.

Millet Packed with magnesium, copper, manganese, and phosphorous, millet can help protect against Type 2 diabetes and support digestive health.

Oats One of the best sources of soluble fibre, oats help to lower cholesterol and leave you feeling energized for hours.

Quinoa Containing all the essential amino acids our bodies need, quinoa is loaded with manganese, magnesium, and phosphorous, all vital for wellbeing.

Rice, black and brown Wholegrains such as rice can help reduce the risk of heart disease. Brown rice is rich in selenium and manganese, while black rice is packed with antioxidants.

Teff The tiny grain with a big nutrient hit, teff has more calcium than any other grain and eight of the nine amino acids essential for muscle recovery and repair.

Tofu, tempeh, and miso Made from soya beans and fermented to maximize their health benefits, these foods are high in complete proteins that contain all of the body's essential amino acids.

Nuts & seeds

Almonds Loaded with more Vitamin E than any other nut, plus bone-friendly calcium, versatile almonds can be flaked, ground, left whole, or even made into milk.

Cashew nuts An abundant source of essential minerals, such as manganese, potassium, iron, magnesium, and zinc.

Chia seeds These tiny seeds contain high levels of omega-3 fatty acids and have five times more calcium than cow's milk. They are rich in antioxidants, anti-inflammatories, and energy-enhancing fibre.

Flaxseeds (linseeds) These are one of the best plant-based sources of omega-3 fatty acids and are high in B vitamins.

Hemp seeds This source of veggie protein helps to regulate energy levels. Hemp seeds are packed with zinc, magnesium, and calcium and are a powerful anti-inflammatory.

Macadamia nuts Packed with healthy fats, these nuts are high in thiamin, manganese, and copper.

Pumpkin seeds These are a source of tryptophan, which is converted by the body into sleep-regulating neurotransmitter, serotonin.

Sesame seeds Full of vitamins, minerals, and phytosterols that aid the immune system, sesame seeds also help to regulate cholesterol and may even help to fight cancer.

Sunflower seeds Packed full of essential amino acids, these seeds are also a rich source of folic acid.

Walnuts Packing a massive protein punch, walnuts are particularly high in cholesterol-lowering compounds, as well as the stress-busting hormone melatonin.

Fruit

Avocado Full of antioxidants, avocados are high in healthy fats, fibre, potassium, vitamin E, and magnesium. They are great for skin.

Banana Rich in potassium and easy to digest, bananas are said to provide instant energy, stabilize blood pressure, and lift depression.

Blueberries and blackberries Filled with antioxidants, fibre, vitamin C, and cancer-fighting compounds, these berries are thought to be good for the heart and to boost eyesight and memory.

Coconut With potent antibacterial, antifungal, and antimicrobial properties, coconut is the richest natural source of lauric acid, which boosts immunity and fights disease.

Goji berries Containing more beta-carotene than any other plant, goji berries also have more iron, gram for gram, than steak.

Lemon and lime Both excellent sources of vitamin C and citric acid, which can aid digestion.

Mango High in amino acids and A and B vitamins, mangoes have antioxidant compounds that are thought to protect against cancer.

Pomegranate Full of potent antioxidants that can protect against heart disease and cancer, this fruit is rich in vitamins A, C, and E.

Tomato Contains lycopene, a powerful antioxidant that may help to protect against cancer, and choline, a nutrient that aids sleep, muscle movement, and memory.

Vegetables

Beetroot Known to lower blood pressure and thought to be a potent detoxifier, beetroot also supports heart health.

Broccoli Protein-rich broccoli is full of vitamins and antioxidants, plus compounds that fight illness, improve reproductive health, and reduce the risk of heart disease.

Carrot Exceptionally high in vitamin A and beta-carotene, carrots are one of the most powerful antioxidants on earth.

Garlic This contains allicin, which has antibacterial, antifungal, and antiviral properties.

Mushrooms All mushrooms are loaded with essential nutrients – many are high in selenium and vitamin D, and shiitake mushrooms contain beta-glucans that boost immune system health.

Red cabbage Rich in a potent antioxidant called anthocyanin, red cabbage is said to support the health of the heart and circulation.

Seaweed Nutrient-rich, low-calorie seaweed is a potent source of iodine, vital for thyroid function.

Spinach Spinach is high in iron, protein, and vitamin C, and rich in beta-carotene for skin health.

Sweet potato A source of fibre, antioxidants, and vitamins A, C, and B, sweet potato helps regulate blood sugar levels and supports skin health.

Other great ingredients

Apple cider vinegar An ancient folk remedy, this vinegar has insulin-regulating properties that help lower blood sugar levels.

Coriander A source of vitamins K, A, and C, coriander leaves and seeds have antioxidant properties.

Dairy Natural yoghurts and cheeses are high in bone and tooth-friendly calcium while probiotics support the digestive and immune system.

Eggs High in protein with 20 amino acids in an easily digestible form, eggs provide every vitamin except vitamin C. A good source of omega-3 fatty acids, essential for a healthy heart and nervous system.

Lean meat Chicken and fish are high in complex proteins, which support muscle recovery and repair. Oily fish are rich in omega-3 fatty acids, which are essential for heart health and for preventing inflammatory diseases.

Olive oil Rich in monounsaturated fatty acids, renowned for their cholesterol-balancing properties.

Raw honey With antibacterial, antifungal, and antiviral properties, raw honey is a powerful natural antioxidant and healer.

Tamari soy sauce A gluten-free soy sauce that provides niacin, manganese, and the mood-enhancing amino acid, tryptophan.

Turmeric A powerful anti-inflammatory and immune booster, turmeric has been used for centuries in Chinese and Indian medicine.

Houmous

Cashew Cream

Hazelnut Dukkah

Beetroot Houmous

Make it or buy it!

These simple favourites add flavour and texture to many of the recipes in the book. You can easily buy them, but homemade is always the best.

Hazelnut Dukkah

Makes approx. 100g (3½oz)
55g (scant 2oz) hazelnuts · 40g (1½oz) sesame seeds · 1 tbsp coriander seeds · 1 tbsp cumin seeds · 1 tsp salt · 1 tsp pepper

1 Preheat the oven to 180°C (350°F), or 160°C (320°F) fan. Roast the nuts on a tray in the oven for 10 minutes.
2 Once cool, rub the nuts to loosen the skins. Put the nuts, seeds, salt, and pepper in a food processor and whizz until finely chopped. Store in an airtight container in the fridge for up to 2 months.

Houmous

Makes approx. 300g (10½oz)
200g (7oz) chickpeas, ready to eat · 2 tbsp lemon juice · 1 clove garlic, crushed · 1 tbsp tahini · ½ tsp salt · 2 tbsp olive oil · 1–3 tbsp filtered water (optional) · Salt and pepper to taste

1 Put all the ingredients, except the oil and water, in a blender and whizz.
2 With the motor running, drizzle the oil, then the water until the desired consistency is reached.
3 Season to taste with more lemon, salt, and pepper. Store in an airtight container in the fridge for 2–3 days.

Beetroot Houmous

Makes approx. 350g (12oz)
100g (3½oz) beetroot, roughly chopped · ½ tbsp olive oil

Place the beetroot on a roasting tray and drizzle with ½ tbsp of oil. Roast for 30 minutes until soft. Follow from Step 1 in houmous recipe (see left).

Cashew Cream

Makes approx. 200g (7oz)
120g (4¼oz) cashew nuts · 120ml (4fl oz) filtered water

1 Soak cashews overnight in double the volume of water. Drain and rinse.

Granola

Sweet Potato Falafels

Pickled Cucumber

2 Put the cashews in a blender with filtered water and whizz until smooth. Store in the fridge in an airtight container for 2-3 days.

Granola

Makes approx. 400g (14oz)
50g (1¾oz) rolled oats • 40g (1½oz) pumpkin seeds • 40g (1½oz) sunflower seeds • 25g (scant 1oz) chia seeds • 35g (1¼oz) walnuts • 35g (1¼oz) whole almonds • 1 tsp cinnamon • 1 tbsp coconut oil • 1 tbsp maple syrup • 65g (2¼oz) dates, destoned and chopped • 30g (1oz) goji berries

1 Preheat the oven to 180°C (350°F) or 160°C (320°F) fan.
2 Combine the oats, seeds, nuts, and cinnamon in a big bowl.
3 Heat the coconut oil and syrup in a pan, then stir this into the dry mixture.
4 Line a baking tray with greaseproof paper, spread out the granola mixture, and bake in the oven for 10 minutes.
5 Remove from the oven, stir well,

and return to the oven for another 10 minutes, until golden.
6 Remove from oven and stir in the dried fruit. Leave to cool. Store in an airtight container for up to 3 months.

Sweet Potato Falafels

Makes 4
50g (1¾oz) sweet potato, skin on and diced • 1 tsp coconut oil • 1 tbsp red onion, finely chopped • 1 clove garlic, crushed • ¼ tsp turmeric • ¼ tsp cumin • ½ tsp red chilli, finely chopped • 50g (1¾oz) chickpeas, ready to eat • 1 tbsp lemon juice • ½ tbsp tahini • 1 tbsp coriander, chopped • Salt and pepper to taste

1 Preheat the oven to 200°C (400°F) or 180°C (350°F) fan.
2 Steam the sweet potato for 10-15 minutes until soft.
3 Heat the oil in a frying pan over a medium heat and fry onions and garlic until soft. Add the spices, then cook for 2 minutes.

4 Put the chickpeas, potato, lemon juice, tahini, and coriander in a food processor and pulse until very roughly combined. Tip into a bowl with the spicy onion mixture and combine.
5 Season with salt and pepper.
6 Roll the mix into four balls, put on a baking tray, and bake for 20 minutes.
7 Leave to cool on a wire rack to firm up before serving.

Pickled Cucumber

Makes approx. 300g (10½oz)
1 cucumber • 1 tsp salt • 1 tsp red chilli, deseeded, finely chopped • 1 tbsp ginger root, peeled and finely chopped • 100ml (3½fl oz) apple cider vinegar • 1 tbsp raw honey

1 Slice the cucumber into strips along its length, making ribbons.
2 Combine all the ingredients in a large bowl. Stir well, cover, and refrigerate for between 30 minutes and 2 hours, while it pickles.
3 Transfer to a glass jar and store in the fridge for up to 2 months.

Kimchi

Chimichurri Sauce

Sweetcorn Salsa

Baba Ganoush

Kimchi

Fills an approx. 1ltr (34fl oz) jar
750ml (25fl oz) filtered water ·
3 tbsp salt · 450g (16oz) red cabbage,
shredded · 100g (3½oz) daikon (or
red) radish, julienned · 1 red chilli,
deseeded, finely chopped · 3 cloves
garlic, crushed · 20g (¾oz) ginger,
grated · 2 spring onions, chopped

1 Sterilize your jar and lid in boiling
water. Leave to dry.
2 Mix the water and salt in a jug.
3 Put the cabbage and radish in a
bowl and cover it with the salty water.
4 Place a plate directly on top of the
cabbage mix to keep it immersed in
brine. Cover with cling film. Leave to
stand overnight at room temperature.
5 Drain the cabbage and radish
reserving the brine. Rinse under cold
running water and return to the bowl.
6 Add the chilli, garlic, ginger, and
spring onions to the bowl and mix
well with the cabbage. Pack the
mixture firmly into the jar by pushing
it down with the back of a spoon.
7 Pour the reserved brine into the
jar until the mixture is just covered.

8 Pop the lid on and leave at room
temperature, out of direct sunlight,
for 1–5 days.
9 Remove the lid each day and push
the mix back down under the brine.
It's ready when you like the taste!
10 Kimchi can be eaten straight away
or left to develop it's distinctive
flavour – deliciously tangy. When it's
right for your tastebuds, transfer to the
fridge, where it will keep for up to 1
month in an airtight container.

Baba Ganoush

Makes approx. 400g (14oz)
1 medium aubergine · 1 clove of
garlic, crushed · 1 tbsp lemon juice
· 60g (2oz) tahini · Salt to taste

1 Heat the oven to 220°C (425°F)
or 200°C (400°F) fan. Place the
aubergine on a baking tray and prick
skin with a fork. Roast for 25 minutes.
2 Peel off the skin while hot and
remove the stem, then roughly chop
the flesh. Put in a food processor with
garlic, lemon, and tahini. Whizz to a
thick purée. Add salt and lemon juice
to taste. Leave to cool.

Chimichurri Sauce

Makes approx. 90g (3oz)
4 cloves garlic, crushed · 40g
(1½oz) parsley, chopped · 2 tsp
dried oregano · 3 tbsp apple cider
vinegar · 4–6 tbsp olive oil

1 Add the ingredients (except the oil)
to the small bowl of a food processor
or blender. Whizz until combined.
2 With the motor running, drizzle in
the oil until smooth. Store in an
airtight container in the fridge for up
to 2 weeks. Shake well before serving.

Sweetcorn Salsa

Makes approx. 600g (21oz)
1 tbsp coconut oil · 1 corn on the
cob · ¼ red onion, finely sliced ·
1 large tomato, diced · 1 tsp red
chilli, deseeded and finely chopped
· ½ lime, juice of · 1 tbsp coriander,
chopped · 1 tsp olive oil · Salt
and pepper to taste

1 Heat the oil in a frying pan over a
high heat. Place the sweetcorn in the
pan and cook until it is just starting to
char, turning frequently.

Harissa Marinade

Guacamole

Balsamic Glaze

Avocado Pesto

Salsa Verde

2 Remove and leave to cool before slicing the kernels off the cob.
3 Add the corn to a bowl with the remaining salsa ingredients, then season with salt and pepper. It is best eaten fresh, but can be stored in the fridge for 1–2 days.

Harissa Marinade

Makes approx. 80g (2¾oz)
1 red pepper, roasted and peeled • 1 tsp cumin seeds • 1 tsp caraway seeds • 1 tbsp olive oil • 1 tbsp lemon juice • 2 cloves garlic, crushed • 1 tsp apple cider vinegar • ¼ tsp salt • ¼ tsp chilli flakes (to taste)

l Heat the oven to 220°C (425°F) or 200°C (400°F) fan. Put the red pepper on a small baking tray and roast for 10–15 minutes, until soft and the skin is blistering. Remove and leave to cool before peeling. Discard the skin and put the flesh and seeds in the small bowl of a food processor.
2 Add the rest of the ingredients and whizz until smooth. Store in an airtight container in the fridge for up to 1 week.

Guacamole

Makes approx. 225g (8oz)
100g (3½oz) avocado flesh • 100g (3½oz) tomato, cored and chopped • 1 tbsp lime juice • ½–1 tsp red chilli, deseeded and finely chopped • 1 garlic clove, crushed • 1 tbsp coriander, chopped • 1 pinch of salt

l Put the ingredients in the small bowl of a food processor and pulse until roughly combined. Keep it chunky!
2 Alternatively, place the avocado in a bowl and mash with a fork. Roughly chop the tomato into small pieces. Add all the other ingredients to the bowl and combine.
3 Best eaten fresh, but can be stored in an airtight container in the fridge overnight.

Balsamic Glaze

Makes approx. 75ml (2½fl oz)
125ml (4¼fl oz) balsamic vinegar

l Pour the vinegar into a small saucepan and bring to the boil.
2 Turn down the heat and simmer, uncovered, for 10–15 minutes, until

the vinegar has reduced to around a quarter in volume, but is still runny.
3 Store in an airtight container for up to 6 months.

Salsa Verde

Makes approx. 250g (9oz)
30g (1oz) coriander • 125g (4½oz) cashew nuts • 4 tbsp lime juice • 1 garlic clove, crushed • 75ml (2½fl oz) water • ¼ tsp salt • 1 tbsp olive oil

l Place the ingredients (except the oil) in a blender. Whizz until combined.
2 With the motor running, drizzle oil in until smooth. Store in an airtight container in the fridge for 1 week.

Avocado Pesto

Makes approx. 150g (5½oz)
100g (3½oz) avocado flesh • 2 tbsp pine nuts • 2 tsp lime juice • 1 clove garlic, crushed • 4 tsp olive oil • 15g (½oz) coriander • Salt to taste

Combine the ingredients in a food processor or blender and whizz until smooth. Store in an airtight container in the fridge for 1–2 days.

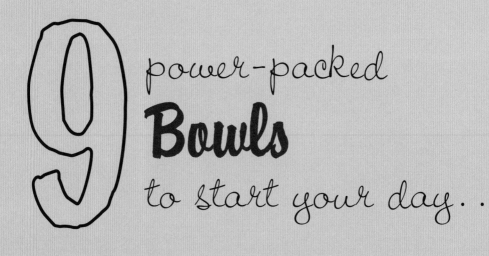

9 power-packed **Bowls** to start your day . . .

Breakfast

Quinoa & berry porridge

Protein and antioxidant packed, this porridge keeps you energized until lunch.

Ingredients

Serves 1

50g (1¾oz) tri-coloured quinoa
250ml (8½fl oz) almond milk
Maple syrup or raw honey to taste
20g (¾oz) blueberries
30g (1oz) raspberries
40g (1½oz) blackberries
1 tbsp dried goji berries
1 tbsp almond flakes
1 tsp golden linseeds (flaxseeds)
1 pinch of ground cinnamon
1 tbsp acai berry powder (optional)

Method

1 To make the quinoa porridge, rinse the quinoa and place in a pan on the hob. Add the almond milk, then bring to the boil.

2 Turn down the heat and simmer, uncovered, for around 25 minutes until the liquid has been absorbed, stirring occasionally.

3 Add maple syrup or honey to taste.

4 Place in a bowl and top with the berries, nuts, and seeds.

5 Sprinkle with a pinch of cinnamon. Add a spoonful of acai berry powder, if desired.

Boost it!

For a mega-antioxidant boost, mix 1 tbsp acai berry powder with your cooked quinoa.

Per serving:
Calories 522 · **Total fat** 31.1g · **Sat. fat** 7.8g · **Protein** 18.8g ·
Carbohydrates 44.5g · **Sugar** 12.3g · **Sodium** 60mg · **Fibre** 16.1g

Sunday prep

Make your quinoa
porridge ahead and
store for up to 4 days in
the fridge. Simply warm
through in a pan before
adding toppings.

Black rice & tropical fruit bowl

Coconut contains lauric acid, which boosts "good" HDL cholesterol levels in the blood.

Ingredients

Serves 1

50g (1¾oz) black rice

30g (1oz) desiccated coconut (or coconut flakes)

200ml (7fl oz) warm water

1 tsp vanilla extract

1 tbsp maple syrup to taste

1 tsp baobab powder (optional)

½ small pineapple, cored and diced, approx. 50g (1¾oz)

¼ mango, sliced

1 passionfruit, scooped out

½ kiwi, sliced

1 tbsp macadamia nuts, lightly toasted and crushed

1 tbsp goji berries

1 tbsp coconut flakes, lightly toasted

1 tbsp cashew cream (optional: see p.12)

Method

1 Soak rice overnight in double the volume of water. Drain and rinse.

2 To make the coconut "milk", put the coconut flakes and warm water in a high-speed blender and leave to sit for 5 minutes, then whizz until smooth and milky.

3 Using a muslin cloth, line a sieve, and strain the milk over a jug.

4 Place 150ml (5fl oz) of homemade coconut milk, the rice, and vanilla extract in a saucepan on the hob and bring to the boil. Reduce the heat and simmer, covered, for 30–40 minutes until the rice is soft, yet chewy, and most of the liquid has been absorbed.

5 Add maple syrup and extra coconut milk to taste, plus baobab powder if using.

6 Load up your bowl with the rice, tropical fruits, macadamia nuts, goji berries, and toasted coconut flakes. Drizzle with cashew cream, if using.

Make it!
Cashew cream
on p.12
Buy it!

Per serving:

Calories 812 · **Total fat** 46g · **Sat. fat** 24.2g · **Protein** 12g

Carbohydrates 94.7g · **Sugar** 49.2g · **Sodium** 94mg · **Fibre** 16.8g

Sunday prep

Make the coconut "milk" in advance and store in an airtight container in the fridge for 2–3 days. Shake before use. The pulp works well in a smoothie.

Savoury oatmeal
power bowl

Oats are full of slow-release energy that will keep you satisfied for hours.

Ingredients

Serves 1

50g (1¾oz) rolled oats
½ tsp ground turmeric
120ml (4fl oz) almond milk
100ml (3½fl oz) filtered water
1 pinch of salt
50g (1¾oz) red cabbage, shredded
40g (1½oz) black beans
1 handful of baby spinach
½ avocado, peeled and sliced
1–2 tsp hazelnut dukkah (see p.12)
Salt and pepper to taste
Sesame oil (optional)

Method

1 Combine the oats in a saucepan on the hob with the turmeric, almond milk, water, and salt. Bring to the boil, then turn down the heat and simmer, uncovered, for 5–7 minutes until the liquid has been absorbed. Take the pan off the heat and leave to one side.

2 Place the red cabbage and beans in the top of a steaming pan. Steam on the hob for 5 minutes.

3 Stir the spinach into the oatmeal, cover, and leave to wilt for around 5 minutes.

4 Place the turmeric and spinach oatmeal in a bowl and top with the cabbage, beans, avocado, and dukkah.

5 Season with salt and pepper, then drizzle with sesame oil, if desired.

Sunday prep

Make your dukkah (see p.12) in advance and store in an airtight container in the fridge for up to 2 months.

Per serving:
Calories 578 · **Total fat** 30.6g · **Sat. fat** 5.5g · **Protein** 19.4g · **Carbohydrates** 61g · **Sugar** 8.9g · **Sodium** 232mg · **Fibre** 18.1g

Make it!

Hazelnut dukkah
on p. 12

Buy it!

Oatmeal *bowls*

Starting your day with a bowlful of oats is a great way to make sure you stay energized all morning. Oats are one of the best sources of soluble fibre, which helps to keep you feeling full and avoid snacking.

Beetroot & apple

Ingredients

40g (1½oz) rolled oats • 125ml (4¼fl oz) almond milk • 125ml (4¼fl oz) filtered water • ½ apple, skin on, grated • 1 tbsp hemp seeds • 1 tsp beetroot powder or 1 tbsp beetroot juice • Raw honey to taste • 1 tsp pistachio nuts, lightly crushed • 1 tsp pumpkin seeds • 1 tsp sunflower seeds • 1 tbsp pomegranate seeds

Method

1 Combine the oats, almond milk, filtered water, apple, hemp seeds, and beetroot powder in a saucepan and bring to the boil.

2 Turn down the heat and simmer, uncovered, for around 5 minutes until the liquid has been absorbed, stirring occasionally. Add more milk if you like it runnier.

3 Add honey to taste.

4 Place the oatmeal in a bowl and top with the nuts and seeds.

Per serving:
Calories 440 • Total fat 23.6g • Sat. fat 2.5g
Protein 17.9g • Carbohydrates 39.1g
Sugar 15.9g • Sodium 33mg • Fibre 7.6g

Tempeh & tomato

Ingredients

½ tbsp tamari soy sauce • 1 tbsp olive oil • ½ tsp sriracha sauce • 1 clove garlic, crushed • ¼ tsp ground cumin • 60g (2oz) tempeh, sliced • 1 tomato, chopped • 2 mushrooms, sliced • 50g (1¾oz) rolled oats • 200ml (7fl oz) water • 1 tbsp houmous • 1 pinch of cayenne pepper • 1 handful of rocket • 1 tbsp flaked almonds, toasted • Salt and pepper to taste

Method

1 Mix together the tamari soy sauce, 1 tsp olive oil, sriracha, garlic, and cumin. Add the tempeh. Marinate for 5 minutes.

2 Heat the rest of the oil in a pan over a medium heat. Add the mushrooms, chopped tomato, and the marinated tempeh. Cook until the veg is starting to soften.

3 Add oats and water to a pan. Simmer for 5 minutes, stirring. Remove from heat. Stir in houmous, a pinch of salt, and cayenne pepper.

4 Pour the oatmeal into a bowl and top with the veg, tempeh, rocket, and toasted almond flakes. Season with salt and pepper and drizzle with olive oil.

Per serving:
Calories 526 • Total fat 31.8g • Sat. fat 3.6g
Protein 24.2g • Carbohydrates 36.4g
Sugar 8.5g • Sodium 342mg • Fibre 10.3g

Amaranth & egg

Ingredients

40g (1½oz) amaranth • 20g (¾oz) rolled oats • 120ml (4fl oz) almond milk • 150ml (5fl oz) water • 1 pinch of salt • 6 asparagus spears, trimmed • 1 free-range egg • 1 small handful micro greens • 1 tsp olive oil • 1–2 tsp hazelnut dukkah (see p.12)

Method

1 Rinse the amaranth and put it in a pan on the hob with the oats, almond milk, water, and salt. Bring to the boil, reduce the heat, and simmer, covered, for 20 minutes until the liquid absorbs. Stir occasionally, adding more water if needed.

2 Steam the asparagus for 3–5 minutes until al dente.

3 Bring a pan of water to the boil, reduce to a simmer, and crack the egg into it. Poach for 2–4 minutes.

4 Pour the amaranth mix into a bowl. Top with the asparagus, egg, and micro greens. Drizzle with oil and sprinkle with dukkah.

Per serving:
Calories 441 • Total fat 20.4g • Sat. fat 12g
Protein 22.7g • Carbohydrates 40.8g
Sugar 5.2g • Sodium 280mg • Fibre 8g

Ancient grains
porridge with pear

Rich in phytonutrients, these ancient supergrains are high in protein for sustained energy.

Ingredients

Serves 1

1 tbsp millet

1 tbsp amaranth

1 tbsp buckwheat groats

1 tbsp quinoa

200ml (7fl oz) almond milk, plus extra if desired

1 small ripe pear, peeled and cored

1 tbsp pomegranate seeds

1 tbsp pistachio nuts, crushed

1 tbsp cashew cream (optional: see p.12)

1 pinch of cinnamon

Raw honey to taste

Method

1 Combine the grains and soak overnight in double the volume of water. In the morning, drain and rinse well.

2 Place the grains in a saucepan with the milk. Bring to the boil, then turn down the heat and simmer gently for 15 minutes, stirring occasionally, until most of the milk is absorbed and the grains are soft – these grains have more texture and "bite" than oats.

3 Add some more milk if you like your porridge a little runnier.

4 Roughly mash half the pear with a fork and stir through the porridge. Cut the remaining pear into chunks.

5 Place the porridge in a bowl and top with the chunks of pear, pomegranate seeds, pistachio nuts, a drizzle of cashew cream, and a pinch of cinnamon.

6 Sweeten with raw honey to taste.

Per serving:
Calories 383 · **Total fat** 13.8g · **Sat. fat** 1.7g · **Protein** 10.5g ·
Carbohydrates 55.6g · **Sugar** 14.1g · **Sodium** 103mg · **Fibre** 6.6g

Make it!

Cashew cream
on p.12

Buy it!

Acai berry & kale
smoothie bowl

With kale, acai berries, and chia seeds this bowl is full of anti-ageing antioxidants.

Ingredients

Serves 1

60g (2oz) frozen blackberries

60g (2oz) frozen blueberries

20g (¾oz) kale, destalked and chopped

45g (1½oz) banana, chopped

75–90ml (2½–3fl oz) nut milk (depending on thickness desired)

1 tbsp acai berry powder

1 tbsp flaxseed powder

1 tbsp chia seeds

Raw honey to taste

2–3 tbsp granola (see p.13)

1 handful of blackberries

1 strawberry, sliced

45g (1½oz) banana, sliced

1 sprig of mint (optional)

Method

1 Put all the ingredients, except the honey, in a high-speed blender or food processor and whizz until smooth. You may need to push the mixture down with a plunger. It should be quite thick and "spoonable".

2 Add raw honey to taste.

3 Transfer to a big bowl and top with granola, berries, banana, and mint, if using.

Make it!
Granola
on p.13
Buy it!

Per serving:
Calories 641 • Total fat 37.4g • Sat. fat 10.2g • Protein 16.6g • Carbohydrates 63.4g • Sugar 38.1g • Sodium 41mg • Fibre 29.2g

Sunday prep

Make your granola (see p.13) in advance and store in an airtight container. Enjoy it with milk, on yoghurt, or with a smoothie bowl.

Raw buckwheat & blueberry bowl

Start your day with a bowl of low-GI buckwheat to help prevent energy spikes.

Ingredients

Serves 1

50g (1¾oz) buckwheat groats

4 tbsp cashew cream (see p.12)

1 tbsp hemp seeds

125g (4½oz) blueberries

½ tsp vanilla extract

50g (1¾oz) banana, chopped

1 tsp maca powder (optional)

Raw honey to taste

1 handful of raspberries

1 tbsp blueberries

1 tbsp cashew nuts

½ tsp bee pollen (optional)

Method

1 To make the buckwheat mix, soak the buckwheat overnight in double the volume of water. Drain and rinse under cold water.

2 Place the buckwheat in a high-speed blender or food processor with 2 tbsp cashew cream, the hemp seeds, blueberries, vanilla extract, banana, and maca, if using. Whizz until smooth and sweeten to taste with raw honey.

3 Spoon the buckwheat mix into a bowl and swirl the rest of the cashew cream through it.

4 Top with fresh raspberries, blueberries, cashew nuts, and a sprinkle of bee pollen, if using.

Make it!
Cashew cream
on p.12
Buy it!

Per serving:

Calories 827 • Total fat 42.3g • Sat. fat 7.1g • Protein 29.9g •
Carbohydrates 89.7g • Sugar 32.5g • Sodium 21mg • Fibre 14.5g

Sunday prep

Make your buckwheat mix ahead and store in an airtight container in the fridge for up to 2 days, ready to be topped with nuts and berries.

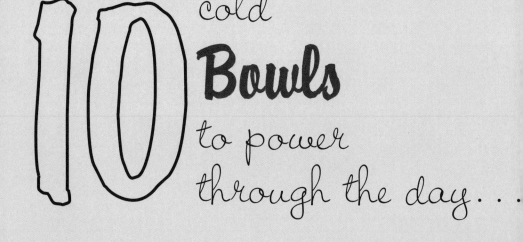

10 cold **Bowls** to power through the day...

Lunch on the go

Vegetarian sushi bowl

Nutritious raw veg and carb-rich rice make this an awesome on-the-go lunch.

Ingredients

Serves 1

50g (1¼oz) brown basmati rice

1 tbsp olive oil

1 tsp sesame oil

1 tbsp tamari soy sauce

1 tsp runny honey

1 tbsp balsamic vinegar

1 tbsp ginger root, peeled and grated

1 garlic clove, crushed

100g (3½oz) cucumber

100g (3½oz) carrot

½ avocado

60g (2oz) beetroot, grated

4 red radishes, sliced

1 small 10x10cm (4x4in) piece of dried nori seaweed, chopped

2 spring onions, finely chopped

1 tsp black sesame seeds

Method

1 Rinse the rice and place in a pan on the hob. Cover with water and bring to the boil. Turn down the heat and simmer, covered, for around 30 minutes until soft. Drain, rinse under cold water, and leave to one side.

2 Prepare the dressing by combining the oils, tamari, honey, vinegar, ginger, and garlic in a small bowl. Whisk and set aside.

3 Leaving the skins on, prepare your vegetables. Create cucumber and carrot "spirals" with a spiralizing machine (or you can grate them if you wish).

4 Peel the avocado and slice the flesh.

5 Arrange the rice, raw veg, avocado, and seaweed in a bowl. Sprinkle with spring onions and sesame seeds, and drizzle with the tamari and ginger dressing.

Boost it!

For a more intense protein boost you could add some slices of smoked salmon.

Per serving:

Calories 657 · **Total fat** 37.9g · **Sat. fat** 6.9g · **Protein** 13.8g
Carbohydrates 68.8g · **Sugar** 22.4g · **Sodium** 651mg · **Fibre** 15.5g

Sunday prep

Make the dressing
in advance and store in
an airtight container
in the fridge for up
to 2 days.

Cauliflower rice
tabouli bowl

Versatile cauliflower makes a great grain-free, low-carb base for this bowl.

Ingredients

Serves 1

6 cherry tomatoes
1 tsp olive oil
Salt and pepper to taste
125g (4½oz) cauliflower, chopped
1 tsp coconut oil
¼ onion, finely sliced
1 clove garlic, crushed
1 tbsp raisins
1 tbsp coriander, chopped
1 tbsp pine nuts
50g (1¾oz) cucumber, sliced
3-4 falafels (shop bought or homemade, see p.13)
1 tbsp pomegranate seeds

DRESSING

1 tbsp olive oil
½ tbsp tahini
½ tbsp lemon juice

Method

1 Preheat the oven to 220°C (425°F), or 200°C (400°F) fan.

2 Slice the tomatoes in half, drizzle with oil, and season. Roast them in the oven for 10 minutes, until soft, but holding their shape.

3 To make the "rice", whizz the cauliflower in a food processor.

4 Heat the coconut oil in a large, lidded frying pan on the hob. Add the onion and garlic. Cook for 3-4 minutes, uncovered, until soft.

5 Add the cauliflower with 1 tbsp water, cover, and cook for 4-5 minutes until the cauliflower is softening, but has "bite". Add the raisins and coriander and stir. Remove from the heat.

6 Toast the pine nuts in a pan for 2-3 minutes until browning.

7 Whisk the dressing ingredients in a small bowl to combine.

8 Place the cauliflower "rice'" in a bowl. Add the cucumber slices, roasted tomatoes, and falafels. Sprinkle with the toasted nuts and pomegranate seeds, then drizzle with the tahini and lemon dressing. Season with salt and pepper.

Make it!
Falafel
on p. 13
Buy it!

Per serving:
Calories 847 · Total fat 60.9g · Sat. fat 11.8g · Protein 22.3g · Carbohydrates 56.8g · Sugar 37.7g · Sodium 184mg · Fibre 15.5g

Sunday prep

Make the cauliflower "rice" in advance and store in an airtight container in the fridge for 3-4 days.

Ahi poke bowl
with seaweed salad

Poke is a Hawaiian raw fish salad. This version uses protein-rich ahi (tuna).

Ingredients

Serves 1

1½ tbsp tamari soy sauce (divided)

2 tsp sesame oil (divided)

1 spring onion, finely chopped

1 tsp sesame seeds

100g (3½oz) sushi-grade tuna, cut into chunks

40g (1½oz) brown rice

1 tbsp olive oil

1 tsp runny honey

1 tbsp balsamic vinegar

1 tbsp ginger root, grated

1 garlic clove, crushed

5g (¼oz) dried seaweed (wakame)

30g (1oz) pickled cucumber (see p.13)

20g (¾oz) carrot, julienned

1 tbsp edamame beans

¼ avocado, peeled and sliced

1 tbsp macadamia nuts, toasted

Method

1 Marinate the tuna by whisking ½ tbsp tamari, 1 tsp sesame oil, the spring onion, and sesame seeds in a shallow dish. Add the tuna to the dish. Cover and chill overnight, or for at least 1 hour.

2 Rinse the rice and place it in a saucepan on the hob. Cover with water and bring to the boil. Lower the heat and simmer, covered, for around 30 minutes until soft. Drain and rinse under cold water.

3 Prepare the dressing by combining 1 tbsp tamari, 1 tsp sesame oil, olive oil, honey, vinegar, ginger and garlic. Whisk and set aside.

4 Prepare the seaweed as per packet instructions. Dried seaweed usually doubles in volume when rehydrated. Drain and chop.

5 Combine the soaked seaweed, cucumber, and carrot in a bowl.

6 Lay a bed of rice in a bowl. Remove the cubes of tuna from the fridge and discard excess marinade. Add tuna cubes, seaweed and cucumber salad, edamame beans, and avocado to the bowl. Sprinkle with lightly crushed macadamia nuts and drizzle with 2–3 tsp of ginger soy dressing.

Make it!

Pickled cucumber
on p.13

Buy it!

Per serving:

Calories 735 · **Total fat** 44.1g · **Sat. fat** 7.7g · **Protein** 35g · **Carbohydrates** 51.8g · **Sugar** 15.4g · **Sodium** 1016mg · **Fibre** 10.5g

Sunday prep

You can marinate the tuna and store overnight, but it must be eaten the following day.

Poke *bowls*

Traditionally made with marinated raw fish, Hawaiian poke is easily adapted. Vegetarians can replace fish with tofu or mushrooms, and enjoy a bowl full of nutrient-dense veggies and fresh flavours.

Vegetable

Ingredients

60ml (2fl oz) fresh lime juice • 1 tbsp apple cider vinegar • 40ml (1½fl oz) tamari soy sauce • 1 tbsp raw honey • 2 pinches of chilli flakes • 50g (1¾oz) black rice, soaked overnight • 1 tsp olive oil • 20g (¾oz) kale, destalked and chopped • 30g (1oz) carrot • 30g (1oz) cucumber • 1 large portobello mushroom, cubed • 50g (1¾oz) baby sweetcorn, julienned • ¼ avocado, diced • 1 tsp sesame seeds, toasted • 1 spring onion, chopped

Method

1 Make the sauce by whisking lime juice, vinegar, tamari soy sauce, honey, and a pinch of chilli flakes. Coat the mushroom with 2 tbsp of sauce. Cover and refrigerate for 1 hour.

2 Place the pre-soaked rice in a pan and cover with water. Bring to the boil, reduce heat, and simmer, covered, for 30 minutes until soft. Drain, rinse in cold water, and set aside.

3 Add the oil to the kale. Rub the kale for 2–5 minutes until it softens and turns bright green.

4 Using a vegetable peeler, slice the carrot and cucumber into thin ribbons. Combine with kale.

5 Layer rice, mushroom, kale salad, sweetcorn, and avocado in a bowl. Drizzle on sauce and top with sesame seeds, spring onion, and chilli flakes.

Per serving:
Calories 536 • **Total fat** 18.5g • **Sat. fat** 3.1g
Protein 16.6g • **Carbohydrates** 80.7g
Sugar 29.5g • **Sodium** 2,152mg • **Fibre** 9.5g

Salmon

Ingredients

½ tbsp tamari soy sauce • 1 tsp sesame oil • 1 tbsp red onion, finely chopped • 1 tsp ginger, grated • 1 spring onion, chopped • 100g (3½oz) sushi-grade salmon fillet, cut into chunks • 40g (1½oz) brown rice • 5g (⅛oz) dried seaweed (arame or hijiki) • 50g (1¾oz) kimchi (see p.14) or raw red cabbage, finely shredded • 30g (1oz) pickled cucumber (see p.13) or raw cucumber julienned • 1 tbsp edamame beans • 2 tsp sesame seeds, toasted • 1 sprig of coriander

Method

1 Whisk the tamari soy sauce, sesame oil, onions, and ginger in a shallow dish. Add the salmon to the marinade and toss to coat the cubes. Cover and refrigerate overnight or for at least 1 hour.

2 Put the rice in a pan, cover with water, and bring to the boil. Reduce heat and simmer, covered, for 30 minutes until soft. Drain and rinse under cold water.

4 Prepare the seaweed as per packet instructions. Dried seaweed needs to be rehydrated and will usually double in volume.

5 Put a bed of rice in a serving bowl. Top with the marinated salmon cubes, the kimchi, cucumber, and beans. Sprinkle with toasted sesame seeds, and garnish with seaweed and coriander.

Per serving:
Calories 489 • Total fat 22.9g • Sat. fat 3.7g
Protein 31.1g • Carbohydrates 40.9g
Sugar 5.7g • Sodium 2,029mg • Fibre 8.7g

Spicy tofu

Ingredients

20g (¾oz) dried kelp noodles (or seaweed spaghetti) • ½ tbsp tamari soy sauce • 1 tsp sesame oil • 1 pinch chilli flakes • 1 tsp ginger root, grated or finely chopped • 1 clove garlic, crushed • 1 tbsp onion, finely chopped • 1 small spring onion, finely chopped • 1 tsp sesame seeds • 100g (3½oz) tofu (firm, plain), cubed • ½ mango, cubed • 20g (¾oz) macadamia nuts, toasted and crushed • Sriracha sauce to taste

Method

1 Cook the noodles as per packet instructions Drain, rinse in cold water, and set aside.

2 Combine the tamari soy sauce, sesame oil, chilli, ginger, garlic, onions, and sesame seeds and whisk.

3 Place the tofu cubes in the sauce and coat well, taking care not to break the tofu. Leave it to marinate for around 15 minutes, gently tossing occasionally.

4 Place the noodles in a serving bowl and top with the marinated tofu, mango, and macadamia nuts. Drizzle with any remaining marinade and sriracha sauce to taste.

Per serving:
Calories 433 • Total fat 25.8g • Sat. fat 3.6g
Protein 14.5g • Carbohydrates 39.5g
Sugar 32.8g • Sodium 446mg • Fibre 6.9g

Tofu & kimchi

bowl

Made with fermented veg, kimchi is full of friendly bacteria to aid digestion.

Ingredients

Serves 1

30g (1oz) black beluga lentils
(or green or brown lentils)

30g (1oz) quinoa

100g (3½oz) firm, plain tofu, sliced

45g (1½oz) thick broccoli stem,
sliced widthways

2 tsp olive oil

2 tsp tamari soy sauce

1½ tsp sesame seeds

65g (2¼oz) mak kimchi (see p.14)

1 baby pak choi, whole

1 sprig of coriander

1 red radish, sliced

Method

1 Soak the lentils and quinoa in separate jars in double the volume of water and leave overnight. Drain and rinse.

2 Preheat the oven to 200°C (400°F), or 180°C (350°F) fan.

3 Place the lentils in a pan on the hob, cover with water, and bring to the boil. Reduce heat and simmer, covered, for 15 minutes. Add the quinoa to the lentils and simmer, covered, for another 10 minutes.

4 Place the tofu slices in one half of a small baking tray and broccoli slices in the other. Drizzle both with olive oil, tamari, and ½ tsp sesame seeds. Put the tray in the oven and bake for 10–15 minutes.

5 Place the pak choi in the top of a steamer pan and steam lightly for 5–8 minutes until tender.

6 Drain the quinoa and lentils and place in a bowl. Top with the kimchi, pak choi, broccoli, and tofu. Garnish with coriander, the remaining sesame seeds, and slices of radish.

Instead of:

Kimchi

Switch it!

Steamed cabbage

Per serving:

Calories 398 · **Total fat** 17.3g · **Sat. fat** 2.3g · **Protein** 25.3g
Carbohydrates 37g · **Sugar** 5.9g · **Sodium** 2,079mg · **Fibre** 8.2g

Make it!

Mak kimchi
on p.14

Buy it!

Buckwheat
& baba ganoush

Baba ganoush is a traditional Middle-Eastern dip made from fibre-rich aubergines.

Ingredients

Serves 1

50g (1¾oz) buckwheat groats

1 tbsp raisins

1 tbsp parsley, chopped

3 tbsp natural yoghurt

1 tbsp lemon juice

Salt and pepper to taste

1 small eating apple, thinly sliced

3 tbsp sprouted seeds or pulses (for example mung or chickpea)

1 handful of mixed baby salad leaves

2 tbsp aubergine baba ganoush (see p.14)

1 walnut

Method

1 Soak the buckwheat overnight in double the volume of water. Drain, rinse, and place in a saucepan. Cover with water and bring to the boil.

2 Lower the heat and simmer, covered, for 10 minutes until al dente. Drain and place in a mixing bowl.

3 Add the raisins and parsley to the buckwheat and combine.

4 Prepare the dressing by combining the yoghurt with lemon juice and a little salt and pepper.

5 Place a bed of buckwheat in a bowl and top with the apple slices, sprouted seeds, and green salad.

6 Finish with a generous dollop of baba ganoush, one whole walnut, and a drizzle of yoghurt dressing.

7 Season with salt and pepper.

Per serving:

Calories 648 · Total fat 33.4g · Sat. fat 4.3g · Protein 15.1g · Carbohydrates 76.4g · Sugar 33.7g · Sodium 59mg · Fibre 7.8g

Make it!

Baba ganoush
on p.14

Buy it!

Tex-Mex salad
& sweetcorn salsa

High in protein and fibre, beans make you feel full and keep hunger at bay.

Ingredients

Serves 1

1 tbsp olive oil

¼ small onion, finely sliced

1 clove garlic, crushed

¼ tsp cumin seeds

¼ tsp ground coriander

2 tbsp pinto (or borlotti) beans, ready to eat

1–2 handfuls of lettuce

1 carrot, spiralized (or grated)

1 handful of corn chips

¼ avocado, peeled and cubed

4 cherry tomatoes, sliced in half

2–4 tbsp sweetcorn salsa (see p.14)

1 tbsp cotija (or Parmesan) cheese, grated

2 tbsp chimichurri sauce (see p.14)

Method

1 Make the sauce by gently heating the olive oil in a frying pan on the hob over a medium heat. Add the onion and garlic and cook until soft before adding the spices and beans. Heat through for 5–10 minutes until soft, remove from the hob, and leave to one side.

2 Arrange a bed of lettuce in a bowl and add the carrot, corn chips, avocado, tomatoes, and beans.

3 Top with sweetcorn salsa and grated cheese.

4 Drizzle with chimichurri sauce.

Sunday prep

Make the sauce and the salsa (see p.14) ahead. The sauce keeps for 3–4 days, the salsa for 1–2. Store in airtight containers in the fridge.

Per serving:
Calories 444 · Total fat 32.4g · Sat. fat 9.6g · Protein 14.7g · Carbohydrates 25.3g · Sugar 11.7g · Sodium 342mg · Fibre 10.6g

Make it!
Chimichurri sauce
on p.14
Buy it!

Make it!
Sweetcorn salsa
on p.14
Buy it!

Millet Buddha bowl
with beetroot houmous

This bowl is piled with nutrient-dense raw veg and rounded like Buddha's belly!

Ingredients

Serves 1

50g (1¾oz) millet

1 sweetcorn on the cob

1 tbsp olive oil

2 tsp balsamic vinegar

1 small handful of baby spinach

1 handful of pea shoots (or baby salad leaves)

50g (1¾oz) cannellini beans, ready to eat

2 chestnut mushrooms, sliced

1 small carrot, julienned or grated

½ small mango, peeled and diced

3 tbsp beetroot houmous (see p.12)

1 tbsp sunflower seeds

2 lime wedges to serve

Salt and pepper to taste

Method

1 Soak the millet overnight in double the volume of water. Drain and rinse well.

2 Place the millet in a saucepan on the hob. Cover with water and bring to the boil. Lower the heat and simmer for 10 minutes until soft but not mushy. Drain and place in a mixing bowl.

3 Using a sharp knife, slice the corn kernels off the cob and combine with the cooked millet.

4 To make the dressing, combine the olive oil and vinegar in a small dish or glass jar and shake well.

5 Put a bed of millet and sweetcorn in a bowl and arrange the greens, beans, vegetables, and mango around it with a generous dollop of beetroot houmous in the middle.

6 Drizzle with dressing, sprinkle with sunflower seeds, and garnish with lime wedges.

7 Season with salt and pepper.

Per serving:
Calories 600 · **Total fat** 29.1g · **Sat. fat** 3.7g · **Protein** 13g ·
Carbohydrates 71.8g · **Sugar** 18.8g · **Sodium** 303mg · **Fibre** 9.2g

Make it!
Beetroot houmous
on p. 12

Buy it!

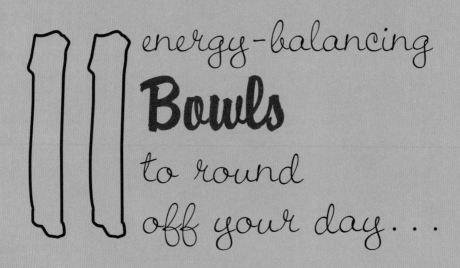

11 energy-balancing **Bowls** to round off your day...

Dinner

Roasted roots & pulses bowl

Vitamin-packed root veg help keep your eyes healthy and lower cholesterol.

Ingredients

Serves 1

100g (3½oz) beetroot
100g (3½oz) carrot
100g (3½oz) celeriac
100g (3½oz) sweet potato
2 tbsp olive oil
½ tsp ground cumin
Salt and pepper to taste
85g (3oz) chickpeas, ready to eat
1 garlic clove, crushed
1 pinch of cayenne pepper
30g (1oz) puy lentils (or green lentils)
25g (scant 1oz) quinoa, rinsed
20g (¾oz) kale leaves, chopped
1 tsp wholegrain mustard
2 tsp raw runny honey
10g (¼oz) rocket
1 tbsp walnut pieces
1 tsp pumpkin seeds

Method

1 Heat your oven to 200°C (400°F), or 180°C (350°F) fan.

2 Leaving the skins on, wash and chop the root veg into equal-sized chunks. Place each of the four root veg in its own quarter of a large roasting tray and drizzle ½ tbsp of the olive oil over the whole lot. Sprinkle with cumin and season with salt and pepper.

3 Roast the chickpeas in a roasting tray with the garlic, ½ tbsp of olive oil. Season with salt and pepper. Place both trays in the oven. Cook the chickpeas for 15 minutes and the veg for 25 minutes.

4 Rinse the lentils and put in a pan. Cover with water and bring to the boil. Reduce heat and simmer, covered, for 10 minutes. Add the quinoa and cook for 5 minutes. Steam the kale over the lentils and quinoa for 5 minutes, until it wilts. Drain the lentils and quinoa.

5 Whisk up 1 tbsp olive oil, the mustard, and honey for the dressing.

6 Layer up lentils and quinoa, veg, rocket, kale, and chickpeas in a bowl. Sprinkle with walnuts and pumpkin seeds, then drizzle with dressing.

Boost it!

For an extra protein fix and some bone-friendly calcium, crumble 50g (1¾oz) feta cheese over your bowl.

Per serving:

Calories 896 · **Total fat** 56.2g · **Sat. fat** 7.4g · **Protein** 18g
Carbohydrates 85.9g · **Sugar** 50.3g · **Sodium** 508mg · **Fibre** 22.3g

Sunday prep

Roast the chickpeas ahead and store in the fridge for 5 days. They make a tasty protein-packed snack, so make a big batch!

Steamed vegetables
& halloumi

Steaming vegetables softens them up but keeps their awesome nutrients intact.

Ingredients

Serves 1

100g (3½oz) sweet potato

50g (1¾oz) tenderstem broccoli

100g (3½oz) red cabbage, shredded

50g (1¾oz) buckwheat groats

25g (scant 1oz) brazil nuts

30g (1oz) fresh basil, roughly chopped

3 tbsp olive oil

1 tbsp apple cider vinegar

1 garlic clove, crushed

2–3 tsp coconut oil

125g (4½oz) halloumi cheese, sliced

2 tbsp houmous (see p.12)

1 tsp chia seeds

2 tbsp pomegranate seeds

Method

1 Leaving the skin on, wash and chop the sweet potato into large chunks. Place in a steaming pan and steam for 10 minutes. Add the broccoli and cabbage and continue steaming the veg for another 5 minutes (try to keep the veg separate), until al dente.

2 Rinse the buckwheat and place in a pan on the hob. Cover with water and bring to the boil. Reduce heat and simmer, covered, for 10 minutes until soft, but not mushy. Drain and leave to one side.

3 Prepare the dressing by combining the brazil nuts, basil, olive oil, vinegar, and garlic in the small bowl of a food processor or blender and whizz until combined. Leave to one side.

4 Heat the coconut oil in a griddle pan or skillet to a high heat. Put the halloumi slices in the pan and cook for 1 minute on each side.

5 Arrange the buckwheat, steamed veg, and halloumi in a bowl and dollop on the houmous.

6 Sprinkle with chia and pomegranate seeds and drizzle with brazil nut and basil dressing.

Make it!

Houmous
on p.12

Buy it!

Per serving:

Calories 1,540 · **Total fat** 104.6g · **Sat. fat** 37g · **Protein** 47.9g
Carbohydrates 92.7g · **Sugar** 19.2g · **Sodium** 1,597mg · **Fibre** 27.6g

Sunday prep

Prepare the buckwheat
and dressing in advance.
Store in separate airtight
containers in the fridge
for around 2 days.

Buckwheat pho
mushroom & mackerel

Pho is a Vietnamese noodle soup with a clear broth, served with fresh herbs.

Ingredients

Serves 1

2 tbsp coconut oil

1 small fresh mackerel fillet, approx. 75g (2½oz), skin on or 75g (2½oz) tinned mackerel, drained weight

50g (1¾oz) buckwheat noodles

1 spring onion, finely chopped (reserve a few green bits to garnish)

1 tsp ginger root, finely chopped

1 garlic clove, crushed

1–2 tsp red chilli, deseeded and finely chopped

50g (1¾oz) shiitake mushrooms, halved or sliced

50g (1¾oz) broccoli, florets and stem, chopped

1 tsp miso paste (brown or white)

1 tsp tamari soy sauce

30g (1oz) yellow pepper, julienned

1 tsp sesame seeds

1 sprig fresh basil

Method

1 Heat 1 tbsp of coconut oil in a frying pan over a medium-hot heat. Add the mackerel, skin-side down, and cook for 4 minutes. Turn and cook for 2 minutes, until cooked through. Remove and leave to cool.

2 Once cool, remove the skin, flake the fish into large chunks and set aside. If using tinned mackerel, drain and flake in the same way.

3 Cook the buckwheat noodles as per packet instructions. Drain, rinse under cold water, and leave to one side.

4 Heat the remaining coconut oil in a pan over a medium heat. Add the onion, ginger, garlic, and chilli. Cook for 1–2 minutes then add the mushrooms and broccoli and cook for 2 more minutes.

5 Dissolve the miso paste in 300ml (10fl oz) boiling water and add to the pan with the tamari. Bring to the boil, reduce heat, and simmer for 5 minutes. Add the noodles, mackerel, and pepper to heat through.

6 Pour into a bowl and top with the sesame seeds, reserved spring onion, and basil.

Boost it!
For an extra protein boost, top your bowl with half a soft-boiled egg.

Per serving:

Calories 648 · **Total fat** 38.8g · **Sat. fat** 22.3g · **Protein** 26.4g
Carbohydrates 47.9g · **Sugar** 6.2g · **Sodium** 399mg · **Fibre** 5.8g

Sunday prep

Prepare ingredients in advance. Put in a heatproof container (exclude coconut oil). Add 300ml (10fl oz) boiling water when you're ready to eat.

Pho
bowls

This traditional Vietnamese soup can be adapted endlessly. All these variations retain the clear broth, noodles, and the seasonings that give pho its distinctive, delicious flavour.

Chicken & Sriracha

Ingredients

1 small chicken fillet • 1 tbsp hoisin sauce • 1 tsp sesame seeds • Approx. 50g (1¾oz) dried brown rice noodles • 1 tbsp coconut oil • 1 spring onion, chopped (plus garnish) • 1 tsp ginger root, finely chopped • 1 garlic clove, crushed • 1–2 tsp red chilli, deseeded, finely chopped • 30g (1oz) green beans, julienned • 1 tsp miso paste • 1 tsp tamari soy sauce • 30g (1oz) bean sprouts • 1 tbsp fresh basil • 1 tbsp cashews, toasted, crushed • 1 radish, sliced • Sriracha sauce to taste • 1 lime wedge

Method

1 Preheat oven to 200°C (400°F) or 180°C (350°F) fan. Rub the chicken with hoisin sauce, sprinkle with sesame seeds, and bake for 10–15 minutes until cooked through. Cool and shred the meat.
2 Cook the noodles as per packet instructions. Drain, rinse in cold water, and set aside.
3 Heat the oil in a pan over a medium heat. Add the onion, ginger, garlic, and chilli. Cook for 1–2 minutes. Add the beans and cook for 2 minutes.
4 Dissolve miso in 300ml (10fl oz) boiling water and add to the pan with the tamari. Bring to the boil, reduce heat, and simmer for 5 minutes. Add 50g (1¾oz) of chicken, the noodles, bean sprouts and basil, then heat through for 1–2 minutes.
5 Put into a bowl, top with cashews, radish, and spring onion. Drizzle on sriracha, serve with lime.

Per serving:
Calories 650 • **Total fat** 26.6g • **Sat. fat** 12.4g
Protein 39.9g • **Carbohydrates** 62.5g
Sugar 10.9g • **Sodium** 1,031mg • **Fibre** 4.1g

Kelp & tofu

Ingredients

Approx. 20g (¾oz) dried kelp noodles (or seaweed spaghetti) • 1 tbsp coconut oil • 1 spring onion, chopped (plus garnish) • 1 tsp ginger root, finely chopped • 1 garlic clove, crushed • 1–2 tsp red chilli, deseeded, finely chopped • 50g (1¾oz) carrots, julienned • 1 small pak choi • 1 stick lemongrass, halved, lightly bashed • 1 tsp miso paste • 1 tsp tamari soy sauce • 50g (1¾oz) firm, plain tofu, cubed • 1 tbsp macadamia nuts, toasted, crushed • 1 sprig of mint

Method

1 Cook the noodles as per packet instructions. Drain, rinse in cold water, and leave to one side.
2 Heat the oil in a pan over a medium heat. Add the onion, ginger, garlic, and chilli. Cook for 1–2 minutes. Add the carrots, pak choi, and lemongrass and cook for 2 more minutes.
3 Dissolve the miso paste in 300ml (10fl oz) boiling water and add to the pan with the tamari soy sauce. Bring to the boil, reduce heat, and simmer for 5 minutes. Add the noodles and tofu and heat through for 1–2 minutes.
4 Remove the lemongrass and discard.
5 Pour into a large serving bowl and top with macadamia nuts, the remaining spring onion, and the mint.

Per serving:
Calories 389 · **Total fat** 33.3g · **Sat. fat** 12.6g
Protein 10.2g · **Carbohydrates** 11.8g
Sugar 7.5g · **Sodium** 543mg · **Fibre** 5g

Egg & prawn

Ingredients

Approx. 50g (1¾oz) egg noodles • 1 tbsp coconut oil • 1 spring onion, finely chopped (plus garnish) • 1 tsp ginger root, finely chopped • 1 garlic clove, crushed • 1–2 tsp red chilli, deseeded, finely chopped • 15g (½oz) kale, destalked, chopped • 5g (⅛oz) dried dulce seaweed • 1 tsp miso paste • 1 tsp tamari soy sauce • 50g (1¾oz) king prawns, ready to eat • 1 tbsp fresh coriander, chopped (plus garnish) • ¼ small mango, diced • 1 tbsp peanuts, toasted, crushed • 1 lemon wedge

Method

1 Cook the noodles as per packet instructions. Drain, rinse in cold water, and set aside.
2 Heat the oil in a pan over a medium heat. Add the spring onion, ginger, garlic, and chilli. Cook for 1–2 minutes. Add the kale and dulce seaweed and cook for 2 more minutes.
3 Dissolve the miso paste in 300ml (10fl oz) boiling water and add to the pan with the tamari soy sauce. Bring to the boil, reduce heat, and simmer for 5 minutes. Add the noodles, prawns, and coriander and heat through for 1–2 minutes.
4 Pour into a large serving bowl and top with the mango, peanuts, the remaining spring onion, and a sprig of coriander. Serve with the lemon wedge on the side.

Per serving:
Calories 505 · **Total fat** 22.7g · **Sat. fat** 12g
Protein 22.7g · **Carbohydrates** 56.1g
Sugar 17g · **Sodium** 812mg · **Fibre** 6.9g

Spicy harissa chicken & rice bowl

Chicken is full of protein, which your body needs for growth and repair.

Ingredients

Serves 1

1 chicken breast or thigh, cut into chunks

2 tbsp (1¾oz) harissa marinade (see p.15)

50g (1¾oz) brown basmati rice

1 pinch of salt

1 tbsp olive oil

½ red pepper, sliced

½ courgette, sliced

20g (¾oz) kale, destalked and chopped

1–2 tbsp salsa verde (see p.15)

1 tbsp flaked almonds, lightly toasted

Salt and pepper to taste

Method

1 Preheat the oven to 200°C (400°F), or 180°C (350°F) fan.

2 Place the chicken in a bowl with the harissa and leave to marinate while you prepare the rice and chop the veg.

3 Rinse the rice and place in a pan on the hob. Cover with water and bring to the boil with a pinch of salt. Turn down the heat and simmer for 30 minutes until the rice is soft.

4 Spread the chicken chunks on a baking tray and place in the oven for 10–15 minutes until cooked through.

5 Heat the olive oil in a griddle pan over a medium-high heat. Add the pepper, courgette, and kale to the pan and cook until the veg are softening – around 5 minutes.

6 Drain the rice and place in a serving bowl with the spicy chicken chunks and griddled veg. Serve with a heap of salsa verde and sprinkle with toasted almond flakes. Season with salt and pepper.

Make it!

Salsa verde
on p.15

Buy it!

Per serving:

Calories 733 · **Total fat** 35.8g · **Sat. fat** 5.2g · **Protein** 50.5g

Carbohydrates 58g · **Sugar** 12.8g · **Sodium** 429mg · **Fibre** 6.9g

Make it!

Harissa
on p.15

Buy it!

Courgetti
& roasted chickpeas

Chickpeas are a great source of zinc, which supports your immune system.

Ingredients

Serves 1

100g (3½oz) carrot, roughly chopped

1 tbsp olive oil

1 clove garlic, crushed

¼ tsp ground cumin

Cayenne pepper, a generous pinch

¼ tsp ground turmeric

Salt and pepper

100g (3½oz) chickpeas, ready to eat

30g (1oz) kale, destalked and chopped

100g (3½oz) courgette, spiralized

1–2 tbsp avocado pesto, plus extra to top (see p.15)

75g (2½oz) mozzarella, sliced

1–2 tsp balsamic glaze, to taste (see p.15)

1 tbsp pine nuts, toasted

Method

1 Preheat the oven to 200°C (400°F), or 180°C fan (350°F). Spread the carrot on a baking tray and toss with ½ tbsp olive oil, the garlic, cumin, cayenne, and turmeric. Season with salt and pepper. Roast in the oven for 10 minutes.

2 Remove from the oven and toss with the chickpeas, making sure everything is coated in spice. Return to the oven and roast for another 10 minutes.

3 In a small bowl, toss the kale with the remaining oil and a pinch of salt. Scrunch it together with your hands. Remove the baking tray from the oven and add the kale. Roast for another 5 minutes.

4 Place the spiralized courgette in a mixing bowl and cover with boiling water. Blanch for 1 minute, drain, and return to the bowl. Add the pesto and toss with the noodles, then transfer to a serving bowl.

5 Top with the roasted chickpeas, veg, mozzarella, and more pesto. Drizzle with balsamic glaze, sprinkle with pine nuts, and season with salt and pepper.

Make it!

Avocado pesto & balsamic glaze
on p.15

Buy it!

Per serving:
Calories 801 · **Total fat** 62.6g · **Sat. fat** 15.5g · **Protein** 30.6g
Carbohydrates 31.9g · **Sugar** 14.3g · **Sodium** 563mg · **Fibre** 13.2g

Sunday prep

Make the pesto and glaze (see p.15) ahead. The pesto keeps for 1–2 days in the fridge, and the glaze for up to 6 months.

Spiced millet & vegetable bowl

Millet is rich in minerals and B vitamins to keep you feeling energized.

Ingredients

Serves 1

50g (1¾oz) millet flakes
75g (2½oz) butternut squash, cubed
75g (2½oz) tenderstem broccoli
35g (1¼oz) red pepper, sliced
½ tbsp coconut oil
½ tsp each mustard and cumin seeds
¼ onion, sliced
1 clove garlic, crushed
½ tsp green chilli, finely chopped
1 tsp ginger root, peeled and sliced
½ tsp curry powder
175ml (6fl oz) vegetable stock
Salt and pepper to taste
25g (scant 1oz) cashew nuts
3 tbsp natural yoghurt
½ tbsp lime juice
2 tsp coriander, chopped
1 wedge of lime

Method

1 Place the millet flakes in a frying pan. Dry toast them over a high heat for 3–5 minutes until golden. Remove and leave to one side.

2 Put the squash and broccoli in a steaming pan (try to keep them separate) and steam for 4 minutes until softening. Add the red pepper and continue to steam for 1 minute.

3 Heat the oil in another pan over a high heat. Add the mustard and cumin seeds and cook until they start to "pop". Reduce the heat and add the onion, garlic, chilli, and ginger. Cook for 2–3 minutes, stirring until the onion softens. Add curry powder and cook for 2 more minutes.

4 Add the millet flakes and stock to the spicy mixture and cook until the liquid absorbs. Season with a pinch of salt and set aside.

5 Toast the cashews in a frying pan over a high heat for 3–4 minutes.

6 Prepare the dressing by combining the yoghurt and lime juice.

7 Arrange the millet, squash, broccoli, and red pepper in a bowl. Add the nuts and a dollop of dressing. Garnish with coriander and a wedge of lime. Season with salt and pepper to taste.

Per serving:
Calories 569 · **Total fat** 25.2g · **Sat. fat** 9.7g · **Protein** 21.5g
Carbohydrates 67.2g · **Sugar** 19.9g · **Sodium** 1,019mg · **Fibre** 8.1g

Grilled salmon teff & vegetable ribbons

Gluten-free supergrain teff is a great source of protein, iron, and calcium.

Ingredients

Serves 1

½ red pepper, cut lengthways, stalk removed

½ courgette, cut into thin strips

100ml (3½fl oz) olive oil

2 large cloves garlic, peeled and halved

Salt and pepper to taste

50g (1¾oz) teff (brown or white)

200ml (7fl oz) vegetable stock

1 small salmon fillet (skin on or off)

1 tsp capers

1 tbsp chives, chopped

1 sprig dill

1 lemon wedge

Method

1 Preheat the grill to hot. Grill the red pepper skin-side up for around 8 minutes until the skin starts to blister and char. Add the courgette strips and heat for 2 minutes until soft. Remove the veg and leave to one side.

2 Pour the olive oil into a large jar and add the garlic. When cool enough to handle, peel the skin from the red pepper and slice into thin strips. Discard the skin.

3 Add the pepper and courgette strips to the jar. Season with salt and pepper. Cover and marinate in the fridge for at least 1 hour.

4 Place the teff in a saucepan on the hob with the stock and cook for 15 minutes, covered, until all the liquid has been absorbed.

5 Place the salmon fillet under a medium grill and cook for 10–15 minutes turning halfway through. Remove and allow to cool. Peel off the skin if necessary.

6 Once the teff has cooked, fluff up with a fork and place in a bowl. Top with the salmon fillet and the marinated vegetables. Garnish with capers, herbs, and the lemon wedge. Season with salt and pepper.

Per serving:

Calories 1,319 · **Total fat** 113.6g · **Sat. fat** 16.3g · **Protein** 30.1g
Carbohydrates 46.5g · **Sugar** 5.9g · **Sodium** 1,231mg · **Fibre** 6.5g

Spicy black bean
burrito bowl

This Mexican dish is full of fibre and protein to keep you feeling full.

Ingredients

Serves 1

50g (1¾oz) brown basmati rice

½ tbsp coconut oil

¼ onion, finely sliced

1 garlic clove, crushed

1 tsp red chilli, finely chopped

75g (2½oz) black beans, ready to eat

1 tbsp coriander, chopped, plus extra to garnish

6 cherry tomatoes, halved

3–4 tbsp guacamole (see p.15)

2 tbsp sour cream

1 lime wedge

Method

1 Place the rice in a saucepan on the hob, cover with water, and bring to the boil. Lower the heat and simmer, covered, for around 30 minutes until soft.

2 Heat the oil in a frying pan on the hob and add the onion and garlic. Cook for around 5 minutes until softening.

3 Add the chilli and cook for a further 2 minutes.

4 Add the beans and coriander, then cook for another 2 minutes until the beans are warmed through.

5 Drain the rice and place in a bowl.

6 Top with the tomatoes, guacamole, and spicy beans.

7 Drizzle with sour cream and garnish with coriander and a wedge of lime.

Per serving:

Calories 549 · **Total fat** 27.9g · **Sat. fat** 15.3g · **Protein** 12.7g
Carbohydrates 65g · **Sugar** 10g · **Sodium** 338mg · **Fibre** 9g

Make it!

Guacamole
on p.15

Buy it!

Index

Acknowledgments

Kate Turner has been creating deliciously healthy, happy food for herself and her family for years. She loves good, honest, tasty meals that make you feel amazing, are packed full of natural energy, and are quick and easy to prepare. Kate has a degree in health sciences, writes for magazines, and shares ideas on food, gardening, and family life on her blog homegrownkate.com. Other books include *Energy Bites* and *Superfood Breakfasts*, also for DK. Thanks and love go to Stanley, Scarlet, and Tommy for tasting, her Mum for washing up, and her partner Will for everything else.

DK would like to thank: Louisa Carter, Charlotte Simpkins, and Ann Reynolds for recipe testing; Martha Burley for editorial assistance; and Hilary Bird for the index.